Poetic Images: Ten Benches

Words and Photos by

Kimberly Ann Schwarz

Book Design/Layout by Kimberly Ann Schwarz
Adobe InDesign
https://www.adobe.com

Typeset in Adobe Text Pro
Cover Title Typeset in Adobe Handwriting Tiffany

ISBN 978-0-57858116-3

All poems and photographs are originally made
by Kimberly Ann Schwarz
and published for the first time in this book.

First Edition
Copyright © 2019 Kimberly Ann Schwarz
All rights reserved.
No part of this book--poem or photograph--may be reproduced
in any form without permission in writing from the author.

In loving memory of
you, Mom and Dad --
the nucleus for our family.

Contents

Introduction   1

Ten benches   3

Welcome Interludes   9

Walks, Seasoned with Pearl   13

Cat Camels and Other Fit Things   15

My Drug of Choice   19

Timeless Peace   21

Nuclei   23

Ballade of Today's Lesson   25

Invasion   27

Paths   29

About the Author   31

The Ten Poems/The Ten Photos   32

Acknowledgements   33

Published Poems   34

Photos Exhibits/Awards/Published Photos   35

Introduction

Camp Dennison Memorial Park is nestled quietly along The Little Miami River in The Village of Indian Hill, Ohio. Over the years, it became a special place for me. However, I hadn't fully internalized its benefits until I became more involved with my poetry and photography. Welcome, dear reader, to my awakened mind, heart, and spirit through the power of poetic images: the words and the photos.

Ten benches

along the
paved path
that loops
one mile --
I walk
it twice
most days.

I walk
for peace
and clarity;
for light
and fitness;
to remember,
to forget,
and I
walk for
encounters, like

crabapple buds;
seeds growing,
trees dying;
Steve and
dog, Obie --
leashed, unleashed;
squirrels leaping;
monster mowers'
weekly roar;
mother, father
with two
swim-suited children
bicycling, giggling;

rhythmic droplets,
puddles splashing;
ear-budded joggers;
bird choirs,
geese honking;
can't forget
pervasive honeysuckle;
a river --
savage, serene;
a man
and his
golf club --
golf club?
orange, red,
yellow, brown
leaves fluttering
from westerlies;
pair of
chatting women;
crunchy snow
under our
visible breaths,
fleeced coats.

We greet
with either
hellos, woof-woofs,
smiles, silence.

And now

I walk
for poetry
as I
blissfully pass
ten benches
along the
paved path
that loops
one mile...

Welcome Interludes

Steve and
dog, Obie --
retired teacher
and black
lab-mix,
a duo
I welcome
to pause
my two-mile daily walk.

Against Steve's graying hair,
a complementary hue,
as if he's traveled a thousand
miles of glory and gloom.
This husband, father, grandfather
walks from bench to bench -- ten in all --
four times, four miles, every day,
leashed to Obie, if needed.

Against Obie's obsidian fur,
a contrasting color,
as if he stepped into white paint
and used the tip of his tail to finish
the moon on a painting.
He wanders, if unleashed,
on a quest for treasures, like
a deer's femur,
bunnies that scurry away,
a well-worn weathered baseball,
and a hidden coyote.

As we pass each other,

we stop and engage in conversations --
the state of education
tree identification
back pain
comical Obie-isms
and saying good-bye to our dogs.

And when Steve and Obie
aren't around, there may be
Ken and Odin,
Tara and Boz,
or Karen and Zeke.

All welcome interludes for me
since saying good-bye to my Pearl.

Walks, Seasoned with Pearl

Remembered walks of yesterdays --
She barked for joy, her eyes alive.
I captured leaves of dying life,
In time all would be whisked away.

Remembered romps along the path --
She munched the snow, Come play! she said.
I froze the frame of icebound dead,
In time all would escape cold's wrath.

Remembered runs in zones of green --
She yipped and yapped, the ball exposed.
I seized an image of fresh growth,
In time all would reveal the scene.

Remembered rests upon a bench --
She panted, drooled; our walks were brief.
I snapped a shot: a mellow leaf,
In time all would approach the end.

Cat Camels and Other Fit Things

At 59, I finally conceded: I am unfit.

To the park, to the park I embarked:
Habitual walks on a roundabout path,
Past ten benches -- no sitting allowed.
One mile, once. Gradually, twice. My goal: thrice.
Steady, even-paced strides. Focused breathing.
Over snow and ice.
Welcomed Crabapple blooms.
Beat the heat. Felt fit,

And up at six, up at six, the clock ticked:
Downed eight ounces of water.
Rolled out the mat. Focused on the belly.
Levels One and Two --
    Cat Camels, Press-ups, Dead Bugs, Birddogs.
Level Three --
    Tall Planks, Chair Squats, Side Planks.
30 seconds each; three rounds. Steady, gradual.
Recharged for the day. Felt fit,

And cook to eat, cook to eat, goals to meet:
Smaller portions and grain-free.
Focused chewing and healthy fats.
Natural sweets and small-farm meats and veggies.
Eggs Nested in Sautéed Chard and Mushrooms.
Perfect Roasted Chicken, or Poached Salmon.
No-Churn Avocado Ice Cream. Apples, oranges.
Burps and smiles. Felt fit,

And OUCH! Can't lift my leg.
Can't move, sit, or sleep in certain ways.
Like a dagger piercing my lower back.
Inflamed SI Joint, said the doctor:
    Rest. Ibuprofen. Waist wrap. Cat Camels. *Cat Camels?*

Still at 59, I'm considering: Am I fit to be fit?

My teacher-snarl toward a student in my care.
Self-imposed separation from my siblings.
The disease that thieved my mother's mind.
Another war unfolds in someone's home, city, or country.

        I hear and feel
    the steady one-two beat
  of my footfalls along the path.
    Hypnotic, then narcotic.
      Just what I need
  to restore my sense of self
      within this world.
        Like a video,
  I replay parts of my day
 filled with all kinds of loss --
     mine and others'.

  Soon the birds, the trees,
    the river, the air,
    the life around me
    cause me to pause
  those indelible frames,
 to forget the unforgettable,
if only for two miles worth of footsteps.
   In their medicinal way,
  these walks have become

     My Drug of Choice

Timeless Peace

A life of worth alike the golden fleece,
With all its many truths and myths and lies,
Should steal our hearts to win a timeless peace.

Each day bears witness to death in the streets.
Our guns and knives birth blood, despite outcries.
One's life of worth alike the golden fleece.

Each month, our shouts are cuffed by the police.
We've been accused and punished, but we rise
To aim our hearts to win a timeless peace.

Each year, the bombs bombard by the elites.
Some young, some old have died, all fear the skies.
Our lives of worth alike the golden fleece.

Each decade, we're losing life, claims Greenpeace
And so we must, to foil all life's demise,
Devote our hearts to win a timeless peace.

On walks, I contemplate without caprice:
The loss of life insists that I mobilize.
All life of worth alike the golden fleece
Should gift *all* hearts to win a timeless peace.

Nuclei

Our lives exist within this world of scenes:
The central zone of stars and gas and dust
The bright part with a flaming tail, we've seen
The hub where protons, neutrons charge, a must
Or eyes of storms so calm between great gusts
Or kernels of ideas light up our minds
Or cells, their centers store the details. Just
What if these wonders fail all living kinds?
Like seeds in cores of apples, parents define
A home for their children to gather around
The heart where life unfolds and twines.
Each day revolves, involves, evolves, abounds.
   And when the mother and the father die,
   What now? *We stay or leave* is life's reply.

Ballade of Today's Lesson

My young eye for business garnered me
An internship at Hudson's while attending Owen's.
Five years in management and a two-year degree
And endless working hours, I formed some new notions.
The emptiness I felt despite future promotions
Pushed me to recall an enduring family feature:
The life paths of my great-grandfather and father -- omens?
Like them, I wanted to be a teacher.

Elementary education became my strategy.
I returned to school, dived into the flow and
Hours and hours of study, met a new friend -- coffee.
Learned how to plan lessons for Reading, Math, the oceans
Habitats, the constitution, while going through the motions.
My learning-partner sister and I were eager
To earn the same license driven by our devotions.
Like her, I became a teacher.

My first position was in fifth-grade when I moved to Cincinnati.
Then seven years later, worked with third graders' growing.
After seven more years, second-grade challenges appealed to me.
Days were filled with joys and sorrows, all spiritual explosions
And quiet, collective creations mixed with isolated commotions!
By year 24, with my greatest student challenge, I became weaker
And finally saw through my teaching walls: institutional erosions.
Like others, I began to ask *Should I still be a teacher?*

After 27-plus years and retired now, my life is photography and poems.
To teach and learn with children still reaches deeper
Into the void I once felt -- and my soul remembers, reopens.
Like all of us, I will *always* be a teacher.

Invasion

Oh, Honeysuckle -- it ambushes my nostrils.
Calls Cincinnati one of its homes.
Growth begins in the Spring
And some think it should not, in any season.
Will do its vining in due time -- in our yards, in our parks.
Flowers of yellow and red pal around with white.
It doctors us for inflammation, infection, itching.
I wonder about its role in *A Little Shop of Horrors*
   as a hero, or a fellow villain of the Venus flytrap.
Next year at this time, we will pose our opinions again.
How can it be both loved and hated so?

Nonetheless, I stroll past it --
Eyes closed, mind freed, corners of my lips tilted upward.

- In memory of Mary Oliver, 1935-2019

Paths

The journey
has been
a long one,
footfalls afoot.
Along the way,
she pauses
and seeks to resolve
which way she should go.
Remembering the moment
is only a brief one in time,
she turns to herself
and whispers secrets
into her ear. They are clues
to the illusive
                Whys, Hows, and Wheres.
As answers are unearthed,
she feels some comfort in knowing
she is on a path
that belongs to her.

About the Poet and Photographer

Kimberly Ann Schwarz was born and raised in Bowling Green, Ohio. After completing, first, a business degree (Owen's Technical College), then a degree in elementary education from Bowling Green State University, she moved to the southeastern region of Cincinnati, Ohio, to serve as a teacher. She taught for 27 years in the same elementary school in the regular education classroom. Since June of 2015, after retiring from teaching, she has embarked on the last portion of her life, which includes poetry and photography. She currently lives in Milford, Ohio. Both her poetic and photographic art can be found at the website below:

The Ten Poems:

"Ten benches", Two-Word poetry, October 2018

"Welcome Interludes", Free Verse poetry, January 2019

"Walks, Seasoned with Pearl", Quatrain poetry, December 2018

"Cat Camels and Other Fit Things", Free Verse poetry, December 2018

"My Drug of Choice", Free Verse poetry, February 2019

"Timeless Peace", Villanelle poetry, January 2019

"Nuclei", Spenserian Sonnet poetry, February 2019

"Ballade of Today's Lesson", Ballade poetry, March 2019

"Invasion", Free Verse poetry, May 2019

"Paths", Free Verse poetry, August 2019

The Ten Photos:

Ten benches image #3244, June 2019

Welcome Interludes image #12981, September 2017

Walks, Seasoned with Pearl collage image, 2017 - 2018

Cat Camels and Other Fit Things image #10059, June 2017

My Drug of Choice image #4680, February 2018

Timeless Peace image #3184, March 2016

Nuclei image #13322, September 2017

Ballade of Today's Lesson image #9410, August 2018

Invasion image #13277, September 2017

Paths image #13483, October 2017

*All ten photo images were captured at Camp Dennison Memorial Park, Village of Indian Hill, Ohio, using either Canon EOS 70D, or Fujifilm X-T2 (mirrorless), digital cameras

Acknowledgements

First, I appreciate you, the reader of my book, for wanting to hold this book in your hands.

As a teacher, I brought poetry into my classrooms for 27 years. I had no formal training in the writing of poetry. I knew this writing genre could offer something to my young learners; I knew because it certainly did so for me as an adult. Unfortunately, I missed out on the power of poetry as a child.

So, I read lots of poems to, and with, my students, and helped them write some of their own; just the basic forms of poetry. I want to acknowledge myself and my students and all teachers and students, as both learners and teachers, for the time spent on embracing poetry and its authors within the schools.

It wasn't until after I retired from teaching in 2015 (and discovered the time!) that I realized how much I was lacking as a writer of poetry. The Cincinnati Writers Project, and in particular the poetry branch, became my new go-to resource to learn and understand the craft of writing poetry. We meet twice a month, and share and offer feedback on our poetry.

I thank Jerry Judge, who is the host of this valuable poetry group, for his leadership as a person and as a writer of poetry. There are many members of this group, but I thank the core members who've attended our gatherings since December 2017. I'm not only learning how to write poetry, but also how to offer feedback to my fellow poets.

I thank Mary Nemeth, my fellow teacher and now poet, for her time reading and offering needed suggestions to help my poems look and sound desirable for my audience.

For you, Erin, Marilyn, and Dana, I am so grateful for our years of teaching together, and now as retired book peeps. You are always seeking to experience a new poem from me, and then offering your thoughts and ideas. You build up my confidence!

Finally, I wish to thank my fellow photographer friends from the Click group and from the UGCC group for our gatherings and photo shoots. Many laughs and critical feedback are the needed elements to help me grow as a photographer.

Published Poems

"Peace" by Kimberly Ann Schwarz
*For a Better World 2019 - Poems and Drawings on Peace and Justice
by Greater Cincinnati Artists*
poetry/illustrations anthology, edited by Saad Ghosn
https://sosartcincinnati.com
Cincinnati, Ohio, USA

"Delicious Red Apple" by Kimberly Ann Schwarz
Pegasus poetry journal from Kentucky State Poetry Society
Winter/Spring Issue 2018
edited by Rebecca S. Lindsay
https://www.kystatepoetrysociety.org
Crestview Hills, Kentucky, USA

Pearl Words and Photos by Kimberly Ann Schwarz
© October 2017 (first edition)
© November 2017 (second edition)
self-published in Milford, Ohio, USA
Adobe Ligthroom (Book Module) https://www.adobe.com
Blurb https://www.blurb.com

Poetic Images: The Words
Website Design by Kimberly Ann Schwarz
© 2019 Milford, Ohio, USA
https://www.kaschwarz.com
Website powered by Wix https://www.wix.com

Photo Exhibits/Awards

"Nature in Focus" Exhibit
August 2018 and August 2019
The Cincinnati Nature Center
https://www.cincynature.org
Milford, Ohio, USA

"Minimalism" Exhibit
May 31 - August 24, 2019
Mohawk Gallery/Robin Imaging Services
https://www.robinimaging.com
Cincinnati, Ohio, USA

2018 Cincinnati Nature Center Photo Contest
Third Place in Plants category
Third Place in Animals category
The Cincinnati Nature Center
https://www.cincynature.org
Milford, Ohio, USA

2018 Annual Mexico Beach Contest
Third Place in Flora & Animal Life category
The Mexico Beach Community Development Center
Mexico Beach, Florida, USA
https://mexicobeach.com

Published Photos

Poetic Images: The Photos
Website Design by Kimberly Ann Schwarz
© 2016 - 2019 Milford, Ohio, USA
https://www.kaschwarz.com
Website powered by Smugmug https://www.smugmug.com

www.ingramcontent.com/pod-product-compliance
Lightning Source LLC
Chambersburg PA
CBHW040302010526
44108CB00033B/21